LIFE
in the
SECOND HALF

We Win

By: David K. Jackson

Exulon ELITE

TABLE OF CONTENTS

Chapter 1:

THE KICKOFF

The games of football and basketball usually begin with either a kickoff (football) or a tipoff (basketball). The game of life however, can be a little different. My life began metaphorically speaking with an onside kick. I was born to a teenage mother and father. You could say I was "the son of statistics," because one in three black males born today can expect to spend some time in prison during his lifetime. Black youth are three times as likely to be the victims of robbery and five times more likely to be victims of homicide. Born a black male and born in the cradle of confederacy, the odds weren't favorable if you bet on the outcome of the game, But God! Early on, there were hints of hope or a promise. I was born on my maternal grandfather's birthday and named after my father, who was named after his father. There were whispers that perhaps I was born for good luck and indeed was a gift from God.

Fast-forward to Paris, France; this same "son of statistics" had the honor and privilege of being a member of the Elite Marine Security Guard program. While there, my detachment was the first and only to have ever hosted a Marine Corps Ball in The Eiffel Tower. Luck? No, it's called, "Life in the Second Half." This further led to an early personal discovery. I realized an essential part of the game of life is accepting and learning how to play hurt. "Playing hurt" is a term or phrase that has been coined and used that transcends most games. No matter what game you've played or currently playing, you've either learned to play hurt with pain or you inevitably develop a quitter's mindset. "A winner never quits, yet a quitter never wins." Though we are taught early on to play hurt, pain is as much a part of the first half as victory shall be in the second half. There is, however, a purpose hidden within your pain. Its purpose is to empower, not to imprison you. Yet, if we don't or aren't willing to embrace our pain, we will never inherit or realize our power. From the depths of your pain will arise the greatness of your power.

I know this is the first quarter or the beginning of your transformation, but to survive or succeed in the second half, we have to approach whatever has caused our pain with forthrightness and honesty. In doing so, we might extract our strength and take ownership of the power that awaits us.

We will discover as others will admit and agree, that whoever or whatever angers you also controls you. Take your power back and maintain control in the second half. No matter who or what it was or is, we are on a mission to identify our ITs. We all have an IT, whether IT be a parent, child, spouse, loved one, stranger, friend, or a particular place or a thing. Our IT usually describes those things (such as pain) we pretend never happened or that doesn't exist or happen. Okay, I sense by now you're getting a bit testy. Take a moment and begin to envision yourself overcoming and being *victorious*! Begin saying out loud, "I am a winner. I am a child of destiny." Now read and repeat this affirmation:

It begins today; it begins with me

No longer will I wait; I begin now to say,

Because I know what I say I am going to see.

Because of the Power that God has placed within me.

So I speak life to my every situation,

Not according to how it looks or how it feels

But as it is written in God's will.

The transformation from pain to power commences when we change our views (what we see), our verbiage (what we say), and our values (how we allow others to handle or treat us). By discovering and identifying our pain, we begin laying the foundation for a solid and successful second half or transformation. Remember: no matter what happened yesterday or in your past, today is your second half; an opportunity to begin again and to begin anew.

Let us be mindful that during this acknowledgment process, it could feel unproductive or like a waste of time. Yet experience has taught me that to overcome any challenge, one must admit or acknowledge that the challenge or problem exists. Part of the effect of overcoming the pain and the past is the feeling of relief and release when you've taken your power back. My grandfather, who is my life's inspiration, would often remind me to *never* give up; give out perhaps, but never give up. In Hebrews 12:1, the Apostle Paul reminds us to run the race, for the race isn't geared to the swift, but to he that endures until the end. In the second half, you'll gain energy as well as excitement, in realizing seasons change, regardless of your favorite season (winter, spring, summer, or fall). No season can remain. It is a fact that between eighty-eight to ninety-two days, ready or not, a change of season occurs.

We should approach our life challenges from that perspective, that it's only a season; no matter how good or bad IT is, it's only a season. Let us not forget the butterfly, whose origin was that of a worm, yet its conclusion, or second half, is a beautiful insect in its season. As we transition into the second quarter of life, let's take a moment and reflect on your IT and how you have, or will, overcome IT. Remember your IT usually describes those things (such as pain) we would choose to hide or pretend IT didn't exist or happen. Begin now to say it until you see it.

Whatever it is you desire or hope for, begin now to declare it right where you are. For you have what you say: the power of life and death is in the tongue. Daddy (my grandfather) would often remind me, "Son, big people get big problems and lil' people get lil' problems." For it is certain and it is true nothing precious is ever gained without first enduring a process. Define your problems; never allow your problems to define you.

Chapter 2:

RUN IT ANYWAY

By now we've covered the kickoff or tipoff and you are well on your way down the court or the playing field. One team I had the honor to have played with was coached by one of the most influential men in our city and also a great coach. We also had one of the toughest, fastest, and most talented running backs on our team. In one particular game, the great running back had a subpar outing. In fact, he had lost several fumbles and most of his confidence. As the coach sensed something was wrong, he signaled a timeout, called the team over to the sideline and began to ask the great back a series of questions. One response from the great back was, "Coach, I'm hurting the team and could cause us to lose." The coach looked at him and replied, "Son, I don't care if you fumble twenty times; you are better than anybody on this field." The coach then turned to the opposing team and commenced to tell them the play we were about to run and dared them to stop the play. The great back and the rest of the team looked on in sheer disbelief as someone expressed to the coach the defense now knew the play. The coach gave a life-altering response: "Run it anyway." Welcome To Life In The Second Half!

In life sometimes it feels as if our heavenly coach (God) has given the play he's called for us and our team to our opponent (Satan) and dared him to stop us. Yet like our coach, God realizes and knows our skills and abilities. *Run it anyway.* Not that there was ever any doubt whether the play that had been called would be successful or not. In the second half, we have to have personal belief in not only the play that is called, but in *who* calls the plays. Our ability to execute and perform is according to the skill level that the team owner knew and knows you possess. Before you joined the team or came to camp, the team owner knew you.

Oh, by the way, our team did score and went on to win the game as well as the city championship for that year. That's the mindset and theme of this book: *hope.* The objective is to arm and empower you to not only believe, but also achieve. You got to have or you must adopt "foolish faith." Foolish faith is the kind of faith that empowers you to go for it regardless of your circumstances, while reaching and grasping beyond the extent of your limitations. You must believe and know you are a winner and will win; regardless of what the odds, circumstances, or conditions have predicted. Learn to accept and desire "Betterness" rather than Bitterness. Free yourself by renewing your mind and in turn, transforming your life. We win.

Perhaps by now you're wondering, "When do I arrive or get to this life in the second half?" Ready or not, believe it or not, your second half has already been delivered by D.H.L. No, not the courier company, but D.H.L. meaning Doubters, Haters and Liars. If there were ever motivators for your success, they are: The Doubters who said you wouldn't succeed, The Haters who hate your success, and The Liars who have no option or choice but to lie, because it's hard to handle the truth and argue with results. The results at the end of the second quarter or first half say you're still standing, you're still alive, and change looks good on you.

Your vantage point solely determines your view. It's not what you see, but where you are when you see it. Your vantage point or position has a direct effect on how you see what you see. An analogy comes to mind. While sitting at a table with my uncle, in the center of the table sat a bottle with labels upon it. I asked my uncle to tell me from his position at the table what he saw. My uncle began reading the label from where he was seated. As he read the label, I realized although we saw the same bottle, he saw something totally different than I did across the table. His position offered a different view or vantage point, though we saw the same bottle. As I witnessed my uncle reading the label on the bottle, I began reading the bottle from where I was seated. At this point I began turning the bottle around so my uncle could begin seeing what I had seen as I began to see what he had seen. Though simple as an example, it is also a life lesson. Oftentimes our challenges and defeats can offer powerful nuggets that can empower us when or if we approach them from the perspective of addition and not distractions. Addition, rather than distraction, implies no matter what the event or occurrence is, it is my choice to gain from it rather than choose to allow the act or occurrence to become a distraction. Our challenges are our assignments and not our sentences. Pain is prescribed. When our views of our challenges change, then and only then, are we prepared or ready for our second halves.

Get ready—there are times when we should view our challenges or challengers from another vantage point or perspective. This is not the doorway or an invitation to "the blame game" or to shift responsibility. Now is the time to reclaim your power. Take your power and become power-full. Never allow anyone to determine your value. For he or she who determines your value also computes or determines your worth. We win.

The "three A approach" to your second half is: first, *accept*; second, *admit*; third, *address*. There are circumstances and decisions that we have to take ownership of, for the role that we played in its outcome or existence.

To grow from this reality begins with *acceptance*. No matter your plight or position, for change to begin, you have to *accept* the realness or reality of our position. Once you've *accepted* IT, as the songwriter says, "Accept what god allows, you're better off anyway."

Now we transition to *admitting*. We have to *admit* we allowed IT to direct us rather than us directing IT. At this point, we should then begin to *address* the challenge or circumstances. Whether this occurs mentally, spiritually, physically, emotionally, financially or otherwise. Deal with IT or IT will deal with you, but IT will be dealt with either way.

Regardless of your personal spiritual belief or lack thereof, this is not an attempt to convert you. I simply offer insight based on the results that *faith* and my personal journey have provided me.

I was blessed to travel and live in places as diverse as Montgomery, Alabama; Kitzingen, Germany; Moscow, Russia; Paris, France; and Madrid, Spain, amongst other climates and places. I can honestly say exposure plays a key role in our growth and development. It is, however, from our challenges or perhaps negative experiences we gain our greatest wisdom if we choose. While at The U.S. Embassy in Moscow serving on The Elite Marine Security Guard program ("Embassy Duty"), I had the honor of being acquainted with some of the greatest of the great our nation has to offer. It was while in Moscow that I was honored to have met then heavyweight-boxing champion of the world, Iron Mike Tyson. Tyson or "The Champ" was unbelievably kind and approachable. His personal story had an enormous impact on my life. The Champ expressed to me this world was full of good people, yet also full of good people who choose to make bad choices. "Being good is a choice," he'd go on to say. This side of the champ was rarely witnessed in public. Mike Tyson is a second halfer who overcame tremendous odds to rise to a level where he is now regarded as one of the greatest fighters of all time.

There is a particular story in the Holy Bible that could easily be described as a second half story. In the second book of Samuel, chapter nine, is the story of a young man whose name was Mephibosheth. This young man was the grandson of Saul the king and the son of Jonathan. Jonathan had shown great love, favor, and regard to King David who is the author of this story. This young man had been accidentally dropped at the age of five by a nurse attempting to save his life from enemy soldiers who had come to kill his entire family. While Mephibosheth's family attempted to flee, he was dropped by the person whose intentions were to save him and his family, yet he survived. Injured, but he survived. Limping, but alive. For years this man-child had built-in excuses. It wasn't his fight, or his fault, yet he had fallen. In fact, he had been dropped. Don't we all have built-in or readymade excuses? His excuse was that he was dropped. What is your excuse or reason? We understand it wasn't your fault. Also be reminded in everything we are to give thanks, for this is the will of God in Jesus concerning you. Mephibosheth was dropped acci-dentally. In an attempt or effort to do a good thing, he was left wounded for life. Take a moment and declare, "It is okay. I am renewed and I win."

Mephibosheth was left with a scar for the duration of his life. From this point forward, let us begin now to view our scars as our proof. There are some scars or reminders that until now, we've hidden or attempted to keep secret. Today your pain is transformed into your power or purpose. I believe somewhere along the way, Mephibosheth contended with or confronted his reality. This is where Mephibosheth's life in the second half began. That is the RSVP we are compelled to send to our God letting him know I've gotten my invitation and my intentions are to show up for the party being held in my honor. Why show up on earth, endure all the pain, and then decline an invitation to your second half? All God desires from you is to tell Him you received your invitation. Some were born with IT (generational), others received theirs by accident (like Mephibosheth), and there are others who went out and purchased IT and now pay an expensive price for IT. Yet God created IT with you in mind. It's a set up for your second half.

I can imagine Mephibosheth encouraging himself saying, "I refuse to limp any longer and if I must limp it will be a liberated limp. I will take this pain and make it my power." At that point he engaged the Three A's: *acknowledge, admit,* and *address*. By now David had become King as was prophesied and expected. David was at the height of his reign. Perhaps like you or me, Mephibosheth was at a low point in his life. This can be described as life in the first half. Give out, but never give up. Declare, "It begins today. It begins with me."

At this point God had placed the bloodline of Saul on King David's mind and heart. We can't say or predict whose heart or mind God will place you or your bloodline on. Be assured and know a change is going to come. We win. In your second half, favor awaits your arrival. Tell yourself, "favor is waiting on me. Favor is looking for me. Favor belongs to me." Believe it or not, as we speak, somebody somewhere is assembling a search party right now with one goal in mind. Having nothing but the good and favor with them, they are searching for you. Imagine all this time Mephibosheth (like you), thought he had been cursed or unfortunate. Even today some are guilty of not transforming their pain into power, however the forty-fourth President of The United States did! His mother was a single parent, father had forsaken him as an infant, and his grandparents reared him. Yet President Barack Obama RSVP'd. He made a decision not to miss his own party or throw a pity party. Our President is a poster child for life in the second half. He journeyed to the king's house (The White House), where a place had been prepared especially for him. In its conclusion, long before he arrived at the king's house, Mephibosheth was discussed. Be mindful that the minute, the second, we renew or transform our minds the process to our promise begins to unfold. Understand the closer you get to the promise, the more intensified the battle becomes. We *win*!

While watching a football game notice what the opposition does when their opponent nears the goal line or end zone. The defending coach might call a timeout and send in the biggest and meanest defenders he has to enact what is known as a "goal line stance." Our opponent does the same when we get closer to our promise, yet we are to have faith and confidence in our coach's play calling ability and run IT anyway. Despite his limitations and his past, Mephibosheth answered the call and showed up to meet the king and received his inheritance. Mephibosheth was now in his second half.

Chapter 3:

THE FIRST QUARTER

*J*akes, *Jordan,* and *Jesus*—the three J's. There exists a young man who is considered by many to be one of our day's most influential and progressive Christians, pastor, and preacher. Bishop T.D. Jakes is a second half story. It is amazing when we pause to consider Bishop Jakes is from the state of West Virginia, yet if you were to ask the average person, what is the Bishop's home state? Most would respond Dallas, Texas. Yet there are times in our lives when God has to remove or separate us from the familiar or comfortable things in order to manifest our miracles or second halves. I'm certain there were those who were given opportunities to receive or assist in the ministry of Bishop Jakes. Yet when we think of Bishop Jakes, we think of Texas, not West Virginia. Our Heavenly Father has a place, space, and time that He has tailored for you and your second half. If there are those around you, near you, related to you, or close to you that see you the same way they saw Joseph in the Bible, as a "dreamer" or someone with a fantasy, hang on and hold on. Scripture reminds us if you enter into a city or town, home, relationship, or otherwise and you are not received, shake the dust off of your feet and depart. We believe and declare, "Our God and our gifts will make room." If you can't change them, Father God, change me. Renew my mind or change my location.

The second "J" is considered by most, the greatest basketball player of all time, Michael Jordan. Michael Jordan is also considered a second halfer. After having been cut form a high-school team and winning a national championship on the collegiate level, You would probably conclude he experienced a Second Half. However, his early years in the N.B.A. were not without its fair share of challenges. He was obviously one of the best players of his rookie class, yet Michael Jordan, after having been selected or chosen to participate in the All-Star game, was challenged or frozen out, according to an article written February 12, 1985 by Bob Sakamoto of *The Chicago Tribune*. Mr. Jordan managed to return during the playoffs and produced an awe-inspiring performance.

Though opposition and obstacles appeared, he never wavered or gave up.

There are second half stories everywhere; they have to be recognized. Of course Michael Jordan went on to win six NBA championships, broke many records, And is today regarded as *the* greatest to have ever played the game of basketball. Second half is that new beginning or comeback against the odds.

The final "J" needs no introduction; He's *Jesus*. The great I am. Jesus' story is *the* second half story. We know Jesus was from the town of Nazareth, yet was so clearly rejected, as scripture records in Luke 4:29, "they conspired to throw him from the mountain headlong." Is there any wonder today as we await Jesus' return why Jesus is coming to the New Jerusalem? The 3 J's simply demonstrate to us that no matter where you're from, where you begin, or where you are, your second half is possible. Revisit your dreams, reclaim your vision, and express your joy.

Chapter 4:

WALKING ON DIAMONDS

Keep your receipts. These instructions were given to me by my C.P.A. The receipts would prove invaluable during tax season he said. We should also maintain and keep all of our spiritual receipts. Those are receipts from experiences that cost us a great price (pain). Those spiritual receipts will prove valuable come spiritual tax time. That is the time when we will transform our pain into power. Walking on diamonds. When you live in a world that has a tendency to overlook and disregard true or natural beauty, it should not be difficult to believe people actually walk on diamonds. Yes, people literally walk on diamonds. Imagine there are burglars, thieves, and even robbers seeking and searching for diamonds to steal and yet there are people who walk on unmined diamonds every day. In Sierra Leone, Africa they have no opportunity to meet or come into contact with people or markets that value what they walk on or possess. Those diamonds are worthless to them and they commonly walk on them.

Do you feel as though you are sometimes treated like an unmined diamond? You know, surrounded by people who don't truly know your value or have a clue what you're truly worth? That is why it is imperative you establish and maintain your value and worth. Like the diamonds that are walked upon, it only takes one person to see and declare, "You're valuable." In that instant, your entire life could be transformed. Imagine people struggling to survive and yet walk daily on what thieves in another part of the world are willing to risk both limb and life to get their hands on. It says simply, what you take for granted, someone somewhere would die to possess. Remember: He who determines your value determines your worth. You are priceless because of what you cost.

You will encounter two types of people en route to your second half. The first will be those who will keep a safe enough distance to declare, "I knew it or I told you so," if you don't succeed. The second will be those who will stay close enough to say, "Look what we've done," when you are successful. Keep working! Your responsibility is to remain focused, vigilant, and succeed despite them both. For in the game of life you will always remember those who offered an umbrella during the rain as well as those who did a rain dance before the rain began. The response is to assure you're better for the cause and not bitter because of it. Once again, your vantage point determines your view. It's not what you see; it's how you see it.

Chapter 5:

THE 3-P APPROACH TO YOUR SECOND HALF

I n Africa, there is a proverb that explains every day the gazelle awakens knowing that in order to live, he has to be faster than the fastest lion. Yet the lion awakens everyday knowing that in order to eat/live, he has to be faster than the fastest gazelle. The moral of the story is: *you better be running.* Allow nothing or no one to hinder your progress or block your vision. Be delayed perhaps, but never be denied, but maintain the 3-P's to a successful second half: *preparation process presentation.*

Preparation: Regardless of your desire, goal, dream, or vision. It doesn't matter what it is you intend or hope to do. You must—or better yet—you *should* prepare. After all, failing to prepare is preparing to fail. There is no minimum or median amount of preparation that is standard; it simply depends upon your endeavor and the results you wish to obtain. Identify something (or someone) that has reached success in the area of your pursuit and use them (or that) as a measuring stick to the level of preparation that might be required to achieve like results. Greatness does not come and is not achieved haphazardly. There are countless stories of sacrifices made by those who we regard or consider as the best in their respective disciplines. Stories of late night and isolated lonely days and even lonelier nights. Yet when we inquire, they all agree it was well worth the results. You shouldn't place your goals or dreams in the hands of luck or chance. After all, luck is defined as when preparation meets opportunity.

Process: Between preparation and presentation exist a phenomena entitled process. Process can be likened unto receiving an assignment with a lofty goal as the end result. However, there are no clear cut directions given or prescribed to accomplish your goal. Remember how Moses journeyed to the mountain top, received instructions, was allowed to see the promise land, and then was instantly released to process at the bottom of the mountain. Never lose your promise during your process.

Presentation: After you're prepared and the opportunity arrives, it's time for you to present your ability, skill, or cause to the world. Practice, practice, practice to assure your confidence and belief in your craft or yourself is justified. Be open to criticism, both constructive and critical or negative. This is the incentive or motivation you'll need to continue working. Never become envious or jealous of those who appear to display superior ability or skill. In fact, these should become your allies or comrades. You never gain speed racing against a slower opponent. It's only when you're pushed or challenged beyond your level of comfort that your inner strength is made available. *It begins today. It's hard to argue with results.* Your path to the second half was not easy or an overnight transition. You've got to focus. The worst person to ask for directions is one who is lost. Those who have achieved greatness constantly express sacrifice is a must for success.

Chapter 6:

DEAD END STREETS

Imagine receiving directions or instructions that lead you directly to your dream, destiny, or goal. You're traveling along steady on course when all of a sudden *you* decide to make a turn. Prior to the turn, you notice a sign that reads, "No outlet" or, "Dead-end street." You proceed, despite the sign, confident you'll be fine. You get comfortable after making the turn onto the dead-end street. You begin to notice all kinds of people along the street. You notice houses and cars on the street, though it's still a dead-end street. You continue riding. Mind you, there is nothing to indicate where the road ends or if the end of the street is near. Yet, you can admit you saw the sign that read, "Dead-end street/No outlet." After riding a noticeable distance, you begin to notice people who appear to be lost as well on this dead-end street. There are even people attempting to wave or flag you down, yet you keep rolling. It then occurs to you that although you have no clue who they are, they realize you're on a dead-end street and are aware you don't belong there. The challenge or problem is, *you* haven't realized you don't belong there. It then occurs to you that although you have no clue where or if this road ends, you've gotten away from where you were originally headed.

You now have two options: continue on a road to nowhere that will eventually lead to a dead-end or turn around. Folks, God allows U-turns. Life in the second half can easily be described as making a U-Turn while on a dead-end street or situation. However, you might have to travel a great distance to return to where you originally turned on the dead-end street. There are so many people this scenario accurately describes. People who are in relationships, jobs, and live out their lives knowing exactly where and when they made a wrong turn that will haunt them until they accept God allows U-turns. After all, no matter what happened yesterday, today is your second half. An opportunity to make right your wrongs and win again. Never allow pride or the opinions of others to imprison you that you become hostage to your shortcomings. Every test you fail, you'll be able to take again until you pass the test or get it right. So you've made a bad turn or U-turn or two? So have I and every other human being if they're honest with themselves. The prayer is there is someone in your car or on your team who is bold enough or caring enough to encourage you to turn around. Simply put, you need someone on your team or in your car who can love you enough to tell you the truth until you're either strong enough to love yourself or be honest with yourself.

In the games of football, basketball, baseball, and most other sports, there is a phenomenon known as a "bad play." In life there are also *"bad plays."* In both the games and in life, you have to learn to live beyond the bad plays. Yes, there are times when it feels as if bad plays will cost you the game. Then you begin preparing for the next game or getting ready for the next play. Some of the greatest defensive backs in the game of football will agree in order to be successful in their crafts they've had to possess a short memory and a lot of courage. Why? Because they are required to forget the last play, whether the play was good or bad. They understand the next play was inevitable. Bad plays can and will happen. The question is, how do you respond to them? Don't make it or take it personal. John 14:1 reminds us to let not our heart be troubled, courage is required to remain in the game even after a bad play or a bad loss. After all, quitters never win and winners never quit. Be aware and beware of the individual spirit that finds itself amongst a *team* concept. When broken down into syllables, the word *individual* is: *in* to *divide* you *all*. That is usually what an individual does when they're involved with a team. To function in or as a part of a team requires great maturity, self-confidence, selflessness, sacrifice, and courage. The acronym T.E.A.M. (Together Each Accomplishes More) is in total contrast to the individual and his/her selfish mindset. There exists the possibility of many positions on a team, yet sacrifice and reality must unite and agree. In every young man's heart is a quarterback or a point-guard and in every young lady's heart a beauty queen or cheer captain who was overlooked. Reality dictates someone has to block, someone has to be runner-up in the beauty pageant, or the foundation for the pyramid that wins the cheer competition. Translated: *sacrifice*.

Chapter 7:

UNSUNG HEROES

U nsung heroes, those people who the masses never hear of or recognizes, but without them success would not be. An example that readily comes to mind was during the Civil Rights Movement in The United States, my maternal uncle (Robert Sims, Jr.) was given permission by my grand-parents at age sixteen to participate in the movement. He was dispatched to Anniston, Alabama, by Rev. Richard Boone, who was a lieutenant for Rev. Martin Luther King Jr., to rally and lead the youth in a demonstration for the right to vote. Prior to his arrival, word began to spread that a *man* was en route to cause trouble as an outside agitator. The Anniston branch of the Klu Klux Klan waited at the local greyhound bus terminal for him. The plan was to accost this MAN and lynch him to teach the local black community a lesson. Upon the arrival of the bus, the Klu Klux Klan boarded the bus. My uncle then noticed the disturbance and immediately realized the *man* the Klan was in search of was a sixteen year old teenager from Montgomery, Alabama who barely looked his age. My uncle exited the bus unnoticed by the cowardly mob. He then proceeded to successfully lead the march and left the Klan to find their *man*. There are thousands of stories such as my uncle's that go unrecognized because it was never about the individual; it was about the *team* and the overall advancement of people. In the first half perhaps it was about you. In the second half, make it about the T.E.A.M.! The word MAN was intentionally italicized to place emphasis on the fact that the enemy was in search of an adult black male. Yet in risk of his life, limbs, and liberty, a sixteen year old answered the call to redeem people and change the world. As we look ahead to our second halves, consider this: "We know what history has meant to us, yet what will we mean to history?" You are here for a reason. My purpose is to offer you hope and assist you in defining your purpose.

The first step is becoming comfortable with the mirror. Yes, the mirror. Oftentimes we're more willing to break or ignore what is in the mirror rather than contend with what it takes to change what is in the mirror. It can be done; renew your mind and transform your life. The intent again is not to convert you, but convince you. It is a fact that you will see, reach, meet, and teach people whom I will perhaps never have an opportunity to. Yet it is for this reason and purpose that God made *you*. You are the called right where you are. There is a need or void only you can fulfill. No one's ever said it would be easy, yet many have proven it can be done. *We win.*

Chapter 8:

PENALTIES

There are times when you don't reflect what's around you and what is around you doesn't resemble or reflect you. When you are a winner and you find yourself losing, that is when you should begin to teach losers what it means to win. Always be mindful that *confidence* is quiet or unspoken, not bold or boisterous. Cockiness is easily recognized and is usually loud and disruptive. When in a losing situation, it is important to have good memory and recall what was required of you to have won in your past. These keys or triggers will prove paramount on your path to winning again. Above all, never couple yourself with what it is you are dealing with or going through. For if your circumstances or situation should change and you've become what you've gone through, then who are you?

In the game of life there are penalties, the same as in the games of football, basketball, and most other sports. There are too many penalties to mention or to include them all. However, I have listed a few that are common and familiar to most. In the game of baseball, there are strikes as well as strikeouts. Football has off sides, holding, and encroachment. Basketball offers traveling, technical, and personal fouls. The emphasis here is not on the specific penalties but the impact they have on the *team* or the individual player that has been cited. In extreme and isolated circumstances, there are penalties that can cause you to be kicked out of the game. In life there are also many penalties that can cost many of us and our respective teams losses! Major or minor setbacks can be likened unto penalties. The key is not to dwell on the incident, but acknowledge it and prepare for the next game. Like the sporting games, there are those who live to jeer not to cheer. They're called fans, derived from the word "fanatic." Play anyway. Run it anyway.

Coaching is critical when the team or player appears to have lost focus or is in danger of costing the team. How many of us have held on to bad plays or penalties? Perhaps you walked away with the guilt or embarrassment of letting the team down. Though it may have appeared to cost the team, there is always a promise in your problem. Remember how it felt? Utilize this experience and gain wisdom from it. Endeavor to become *better* not *bitter* and teach others how *not* to cost their teams. Be reminded even in your loss or penalty phase, people are watching *y-o-u* to see how you respond when you're having a bad day or bad play. In the game of hockey, they have a penalty box. The penalty box is where ones who have violated and are penalized are sent to sit for a predetermined period of time, based upon the offense or rule violation. In life we also have a penalty box. Yet, in hockey I've never noticed the players disrobing, quitting, or leaving the arena because they've been penalized. Neither should you quit or give up when you've had the misfortune of having to endure the penalty box (jail, prison, or incarceration). Perhaps this book reaches you as you're in the (or perhaps your own) penalty box. Be encouraged. Never give up. Take the time; never allow the time to take you.

"Off sides" is a familiar term to fans of football. This is usually an indication that the opposition has crossed the line of scrimmage prior to the snap of the football. Though a seemingly small penalty, at the wrong time or area of the field, it could prove costly to your team. Imagine the opposing team is near the goal line (red zone) and you jump off sides. New downs, new life, and new motivation. Your team is now in jeopardy of losing the game as a direct result of your lack of focus or discipline. This is where the benefit of good team-mates or coaching can play key roles in the team and the outcome. Take a minute and consider your team. Are they dependable during crunch time? Are you dependable? Can you count on them? Bad advice or bad coaching given at the wrong time can cost many games to be lost. Yet timely advice and good coaching can also win many victories, both in life and in sporting events.

In addition to coaching, the role of you as a team player as well as your teammates is also important. Preparation again precedes presentation. In other words, what you've prac-ticed is usually what you'll produce in a time of crisis. Be mindful that bad plays will happen. The question is: how will you respond? The first half is nearly over, but there is time to make adjustments. It's called *halftime* or *a break*. After you've been flagged, make sure you observe and recount everything that took place, for there are valuable lessons to be learned. Oftentimes it appears you are at fault, yet it can also be highlights that those around you can use and you can see how they respond to you and for you. During these times, you are empowered to identify and recognize the difference between teammates and scheme-mates. Teammates will encourage you, while scheme-mates will withdraw and begin to retreat in fear that they may be required to sacrifice or dig deeper for the team during this penalty phase. Teammates pick up the slack, knowing the next play is coming and could likely decide the outcome of the game. Whether teammates or scheme-mates, your responsibility is to stay focused, learn from the penalty, and don't personalize it. It is a fact; in life and in sports, bad days, bad plays, setbacks, and penalties will occur. Some will clearly come as a direct result of our lack of discipline. Yet others will happen because of bad officiating. Be mindful and remember you don't call the game, design the plays, or run the clock. Just play to win. It takes more courage, inner, and outer strength to get back up after being knocked down than it does to lay or remain down after being pushed down illegally and crying foul.

Chapter 9:

HALFTIME

Bouncing Back: "Something's come to us, something's come through us but all things come to pass." This statement or cliché alludes directly to the need for short-term memory and the ability to bounce back after the setback. Our direct attachment to things and people are often misplaced by our having overvalued or placed too much emphasis on our perceived ownership or possession of IT or *them*. Indeed it is a *fact* all things come to pass. This statement speaks to the need to have short-term memory and the ability to bounce back after the set back. Our direct attachment to things and people are often misplaced by our having overvalued or placed too much emphasis on our perceived ownership or possession of IT or them. Indeed *all* things have come to pass. Every vehicle in the junkyard was once a thought, vision, or new car. Every tomb or grave represents someone, whether young or old, short or tall, big or small who came, was here, and after a season—passed. Sounds callous or even cold, yet it should assist us in our value placement or priority processing. As we've agreed, you can't miss the next play while complaining about the last or past plays. Reality is, IT has come to pass, like it or not, accept it or not. Therefore, be the best *you* that you can be while there's still time on your clock. No matter what happened yesterday (in the past), today is your second half—a chance and opportunity to begin anew. Our motto is, "We win in the second half." It is therefore incumbent that we have a mindset to move forward, whether it is the greatest play of our lives or the worst play of our career. We have to prepare for the next play.

Chapter 10:

MAKING MONUMENTS OUT OF MOMENTS

T here exist those of us who are guilty of having erected monuments to moments, both good and bad. Translated: we're *stuck*. Still reminiscing about the play, day, or event that we experienced way back when. Sounds humorous, but you know the person or personality I'm referring to. Still at the park, corner store, or wherever the gathering spot may be, telling anyone who will listen about *that* day, night, season, or year. Don't get me wrong; I'm not hating or attempting to deny your moment. We know the story so well after all these years that we can almost tell it verbatim. The challenge is, that wasn't intended to be the *only* moment. It now appears they're stuck or have erected a monument to that moment. Sad commentary when the reality is there was so much more talent and many more moments where that one was discovered. Dig deep, take a good look, and experience the moment once more. Yet, consider what it took, what was required, or what did you do prior to the moment to prepare you in position to make it there? At this point, tell your moment or monument goodbye and prepare for the next great moment. The challenge might be that we lost sight of the fact for every moment—whether bad or good— it was preceded by acts that led to the moment that led to the moment. If it was a negative moment, remember and be prayerful to not repeat it. If it was positive, remember and be prayerful to do what you did to achieve those results. More importantly, if *God* did it once, He can and *will* do it again. *We win.*

As we agree, monuments can become barriers that That hinder us or cause us to become *stuck*. We must acknowledge that being stuck is a symptom of deeper challenges. We've either lost our confidence, our work ethic has diminished, or complacency overcame us unawares. Yet the results will not be to our favor. When these symptoms arrive, we are usually busy reading our *own* news stories. Receiving Accolades from what we perceive as well wishers or under the false impression that this moment will last forever.will last forever.

Symbols and signs are for conscious minds. Symbols are also outer manifestations that arrive with your moment or monument. The crowds, the awards, your name trumpeted about the town, school, or community. These are symbols that should serve as motivation for you to work harder to greater moments. Yet these symbols will later be remembered as the beginning of the sickness of being *stuck*. We will later recall how everyone knew your name, your number, your note (singers) or whatever your moment was. Everybody knew you, or so it felt. Traditions in so many areas and arenas were established with one moment. God moved, manifested a miracle, and someone erected a monument decreeing God would reproduce the same moment every Sunday at 11:00. Let us be mindful *God* is *sovereign* as well as the fact that God created an entire universe, not just our town, city, state, country, but the entire *world*. Yet when the sickness of being *stuck* has set in, we're misled into thinking everything and everyone will remain *stuck* as well.

As you can clearly see, IT is not necessarily so! Everything around us is progressing as it was created to do. Yet the substance of it all is what decision will you make or choose. Powerful decisions can be painful, yet popular decisions aren't usually powerful. Rest assured, if you set your sights for the moon and inadvertently land amongst the stars, you're still better off and further than you were when you began: *stuck*.

For those along the path that you encounter that are contrary to your perspective, remain focused yet operate in and offer compassion. Compassion, simply put, is what Jesus offers you and me everyday. *Mercy* defined is to pity or feel sorry for. That's what Jesus does for us. We win. It is one of the more simple sounding requests one has received. Yet to further examine the plight of our world and the response and reaction to one another denotes a sheer lack of compassion. This game of life or second half that we allude to is not appealing without a compassionate coach or authoritative figure willing to look beyond our worst plays, practices, and first halves and offer a peaceful assurance that the game isn't over until the game clock shows all zeroes. Interpreted: *the end, we win*, I am grateful to the big coaching staff in the sky (Father, Son, Holy Spirit, and the angels) who continue to show compassion, mercy, and grace on us. It's like the story of the king who forgave the debtor his debt that was owed. Yet the forgiven debtor left the king's presence and encountered one who was indebted to him. Rather than forgiving as he had been forgiven, he demanded repayment of the debt immediately. Sounds rather insensitive or callus, yet as we consider our personal circles and beyond, it is frightening when we compare our world to that of the debtor and the king. Even more amazing is the fact that those who are usually most judgmental and debt demanding are, upon further investigation, the ones who have either only recently been forgiven or are in need of forgiveness themselves.

Imagine the teammate who dropped what could have been the winning touchdown pass, missed the game-winning free-throw, or misspelled a simple word that could've won the spelling bee, or whatever curve ball the game of life has or will throw. It is at this moment that compassion from the team or coach is not only needed, but necessary and welcomed. It is also at this moment that negative thoughts are permeating in our own and hearts and minds. Emotions are high. We are transfixed in the moment. Yet you are challenged to think of how you would want to be treated when or if your day comes. Simply, treat others as God has treated you or you would desire others to treat you. The ungrateful servant fell into the grasp of spiritual amnesia. Spiritual amnesia simply means you temporarily choose to forget where and what God's grace and mercy has done for you. It could easily be interpreted as selfishness or the indirect effect of past pain or adversity.

There are advantages in your adversity, if only we would seek them out. When we revisit the question, "When or where does my second half begin?" we are led directly to the Holy Bible in Hebrews 11:1, which begins with one amazing word as well as the answer to your question. That word is *now*.

The text opens, declaring, "Now faith is the substance." Interpreted: right now your faith is the key to your second half. This is why we declare it begins today and it begins with me. It is vitally important you approach your second half as if it's your last dance at the VIP celebration thrown in your honor. Here's the bigger picture: God has allowed you into a place of pardon and you've decided to slam the door shut. Although this sounds rather humorous, this is the view and opinion that "the hip-hop generation or "the world" has of the church. This mindset and spirit of selfishness is a direct contributor to the stagnation or "the stuck syndrome." Again this is not an attempt to convert you, however, this is an effort to convince you that your greatest moment is yet to come. Begin placing the distractions in their proper place and let's prepare for victory. After all, we win.

If by now you haven't noticed the most important trans-formation necessary for an incredible second half is the trans-formation or changing of your mind. Once you determine you're prepared, begin by feeding your mind. The positive books, DVDs, or people are all ingredients that can play an affective role. The most important person however is *y-o-u*. You've got to know you were created with *your* purpose in mind. The challenge is to discover *you* and all that pertains to you. Learn to love *you* as a foundation and practice to love others. Now is the time that your faith and belief in God, as well as yourself, will be the fuel necessary for this life-altering journey. Please be reminded after your second half begins, you will never be the same again. After all, it wasn't until after the prodigal son of the Bible came to himself was he prepared and had a mindset to return to his father's house. There is a place within every human being that must be experienced to qualify and prepare you for the right to return to the Father's house. Yes, I'm certain there is contention with that statement. However, that statement could be the key to the endless list of challenges that permeate our world. There are too many people in leadership roles in religious institutions routinely who have refused to "come to themselves." They go to buildings, to other people's business, they have come to others and have been in close proximity with those who have come to themselves and would have you to believe their testimony is based upon what they've heard or witnessed. Yet the fact still and will remain: "When He came to Himself, then He returned to the Father's house". It should therefore be no surprise the major emphasis would certainly be the focus of another's life. For when you and I, like the prodigal son, come to ourselves, then *we* can return to the Father's house. It is upon returning (mindset/spirit) that we discover what value and beauty we overlooked by departing. Be mindful Jesus assured Simon Peter that Satan desired him, yet after the conversion, go back and strengthen thou brethren. He returned.

Ephesians 2:12-13 says at one time we were without Christ, having no hope. Verse thirteen begins declaring, "But now, in Christ Jesus ye who were afar off are made nigh by the blood of Christ." Life in the second half can be summed up simply with those two words, "but now." There are those in your first half (past) whose roles as advocates of Beelzebub are to remind you to remain stuck in your pain. Be mindful that only Satan can remind you of your past, for it is God who controls the future. Our assignment is to shift the focus to the "but now" or second half phase of your life. When you renew your mind, God will transform your life. Welcome to life in the second half! "But now" should be your response when the tempter comes to distract or delay bot h your vision and dreams. No matter what happened yesterday, *but now*, it is your second half.

As you're transforming, be aware that just as there were those who condemned you for not transforming or changing, there will also be those who will challenge how, where, and why you've transformed or changed. Yes I agree, yet be comforted Jesus the Christ encountered this same Spirit that was prevalent amongst the scribes and Pharisees. In Matthew 15:8-9, Jesus points out, "This people," according to Esaias. Notice Jesus did not say, "God's people" or "My people." "They draw nigh to me with their mouths and lips, but their hearts are far from me."

Verse nine declares, "In vain they do worship me [Jesus] teaching for doctrine the commandments of men." That entire exchange began because "church folk" attempted to point out followers of Christ for not washing their hands prior to dinner. Yet, they dared to quote scripture to condemn, when the same scripture could have been utilized to set captives free. Life in the second half, your *but now* is right *now*! You've come this far; don't give up now. There are more for you than are against you. Greater is He that is in us than He that is in the world.

Remember Peter did return after the conversion, and was uniquely qualified to strengthen the brethren. Jesus demanded Peter "go back," but only after the conversion. That was a personal and powerful challenge. The key is personal and eerily similar to the "pig pen" experience that the aforementioned prodigal son endured.

As we approach life in the second half from a team perspective, it is nevertheless a personal journey that is required of each and every teammate or believer. Unfortunately we (or the team) can only be as strong as our weakest teammate. So we should be encouraged as well as encourage others to get excited about this new season or second half. Romans 8:31 reminds us, "if God be for us, who can be against us?" Remember IT begins *today;* IT begins with *me* (you).

The empowerment one receives when the revelation or reality of what we've endured is found to be a divine part of the destiny God has for you. Abraham, Moses, and others were pulled or called from places or positions of comfort to begin their transformation. God in fact calls us from our comfort to desert or barren places. Few would readily admit, although they should, that prior to seasons of favor, blessings, overflow, and abundance, there were days of discomfort and lack of concern as if God had forgotten them. God pours in you all that will be necessary to sustain you through this transition. Elisha, while at the brook, was provided for during his brook season, yet when that season was over, God prepared him for his ultimate purpose as related to His kingdom and will. That mindset you're in is only preparation for the greater place you're destined for.

The body of Christ (the church), Christians, believers, saints, or however you choose to describe yourself, is facing a season similar to the time when David was called upon to face Goliath. The climate was similar in that no one in David's time was *willing* to face or fight "the giant" because the giant had a history of having defeated all that had dared to battle or fight against him. Today we are faced with our day's unique "giants" that are garnering their own record of victories and appear undefeatable. Fear of the giant. Though our giants are mainly spiritual, there exist physical and mental giants also. In this world, the giants of sexism, classism, racism, depression, fornication, adultery, alternative lifestyles, lying, deceit, murder, and in general *sin,* as well as abominations. Self-examination is the beginning of discovering how deeply rooted and problematic self-hatred, along with its root causes, tentacles, and fruit is. As believers, it should be disturbing that the view of the "church" is described by the young, hip hop generation as judgmental, political, hypocritical, homophobic, and downright old fashioned. "Amongst young people (aged 16-29), forty-nine percent have a negative view of evangelical Christians and only three percent have positive or 'good' impressions" (www.crosswalk.com). To those of us who have grown or have gotten comfortable inside the four walls, this should be an alarming indictment. When we are reminded that we too desired a second half (new start), second chance, new leaf, or whatever descriptive term you endeavor to use, it was never the fact that David defeated the giant as much as was his willingness to show up for the fight. God simply needs believers who aren't dismayed by the giants of our day, but are willing to show up.

Chapter 11:

DISCOVERY BEFORE RECOVERY

Scripture records, "All things work together for the good of those that are called according to His purpose." Being mindful that the "all" that is mentioned includes those moments, days, places, people, and in general, negative events that transpire in our lives. It is this transition that is set in motion to direct or align us with the purpose for which God has created us. Remember, from your greatest pain comes your greatest power. Unfortunately, Few people are willing to accept that God has trusted you with pain. He desires to exchange your pain for power when you are transformed. The transformation will not occur without S-E-L-F discovery: Spirituality, Enlightenment, Love, and Freedom.

Spirituality: a relationship with God through Jesus Christ is the beginning. They who worship me must worship me in spirit and in truth.

Enlightenment: This is the place where you release it back to God. "Come unto me all ye that labor and are heavy laden and I will give you rest."

Love: The personification of love is expressed and defined in John 3:16 where God expresses what love is and what love does. It gives. As well as 1 Corinthians 13 where God, via the Apostle Paul, expresses what love (charity) is not.

Freedom: He or She whom the Son sets free is free indeed. Once you discover your (IT) pain, release it to God. He releases you from it and it from you. You then become enlightened (or will have gained the wisdom) from the experience. You should begin to love all that God has kept or saved you to be. You are then converted or free.

Hopefully, at this point it is apparent to you that yours, my, or anyone's second half is not automatic or without enduring a process.

The hope, prayer, and belief is it is worth it. No matter how well you prepare for the game or perhaps have planned, rest assured that following half time the second half is coming and the game must be completed. You were born, prepared, and equipped to win.

Chapter 12:

THE ADVANTAGES OF ADVERSITY

A dversity in its basic definition is defined as difficulty or misfortune. Yet when we consider adversity from the posture of empowerment rather than imprisonment, we begin the process toward progress. Consider this: "Our good times with God prepare us for our tough times for Him." In Jeremiah 1:5, God informs Jeremiah that before he was formed in his mother's womb, He knew him. This serves as a reminder and forewarning that God knew every detail of Jeremiah's, yours, as well as my existence of life on this planet. Job declared, "A man born of a woman is of a few days but full of trouble." However, I don't recall reading anywhere where he suggested quitting was an option. In fact, Job went on to declare, "Though He slay me yet will I trust Him.

I'm going to wait until my change comes." Job understood the advantages in adversity.

Perhaps you're wondering where or how is there an advantage in your adversity. Rest assured God often uses adversity to:

1) Reveal what is hidden in you (character/who you are)
2) Reveal who or what is around you (your circle/peers)
3) Reveal whose you are!

Job found himself in the midst of trials, yet God had already revealed He knew Job. Yet there were those with Job who God didn't know and they didn't know God. Job's wife revealed her relationship with God or lack thereof when she advised Job to curse God and die. Job's friends showed up shortly thereafter and were also exposed for their lack of a relationship with God. Is it not amazing that the story concludes with God admonishing Job's friends to go to him and ask forgiveness, and if Job doesn't forgive them, God explained He would kill them. There are indeed advantages in adversity.

Therefore *when* not *if* you are challenged with adversity, pause and ask yourself, "What can I learn from this?" And, "What can I teach from this?" These two questions should also reaffirm or serve to remind us it is not about us. Adversity is intended to propel us forward as it prepares us for promotion. All things work together for the good of those who love the Lord and are called according to God's purpose. The stronger you become, the more your surroundings will begin to reflect the new (or second half) you. There are games and times when overtime or extra innings are necessary. Life can dictate more time or perhaps the time hasn't arrived. I am of the belief God reserves overtime or extra innings in this game of life for Him. While having my lawn landscaped, I noticed the beauty of the grass and asked the landscaper what caused the weeds to die. Thinking he'd name a chemical or special solution, he simply replied, "Sir, good grass chokes out bad weed. When it grows strong, the weeds cannot survive."

You know those moments when friends and family have walked away, or when the doctor shakes his head and turns and walks away. It is usually at these times when it's over that God steps in. When Jesus received word His friend Lazarus was sick, this could be likened unto the game in the final inning. When word was sent that Lazarus was dead, that was the end of regulation. When Jesus showed up, that can be considered overtime or extra innings. Jesus only departed to that place where Lazarus had been laid when he was not only dead, but buried. One of the more remarkable things that occurred upon His arrival was Jesus' prayer. Jesus cried out, "Father I know you hear me, but for the sake of those who don't believe." What that says to us is there is a place for doubters, naysayers, and non-believers in life. Ask yourself what would the world be like without doubters, haters, and liars. Jesus went on to order reserve seating for the making or performance of Lazarus' miracle. There are situations that God will strategically place us in to allow doubters to be assembled. Once they're in place, then the conversion of doubting Thomas' children begins. Another crowd converted. Another game won in extra innings. Life in the second half.

In your quest for life in the second half, be reminded nothing precious is ever gained without first enduring *process*. Like that strong grass that has outgrown the weed that had once overtaken it, grow strong and grow upward.

A key to a successful second half is acquiring the skill to live beyond the offence. Living beyond what has offended you, and letting it go! Forgive if you desire forgiveness. Remembering takes you to that bridge called destiny, yet it is forgiveness that allows you to cross. So many talented and gifted people live frustrated and underachieved lives because of their inability to forgive. There is power in forgiving.

The ability to recognize the faults of others can either be an asset and or a liability. Scripture reminds us there would be those who would have eyes and cannot see, ears and cannot hear, but your eyes are blessed. Have you ever asked why some eyes and ears could be blessed and others not? The asset is you are allowed to see or hear because it is a responsibility of yours to serve as an intercessor to ask God into whatever situation he has *allowed or permitted* you to experience. We are reminded *all* things work together for the good of those who are called according to God's purpose.

Frederick Douglass, the great abolitionist and freedom fighter, said, "God has no eyes except your eyes, God has no ears except your ears; so if it is to be done God has to use you to get it done." The liability is that if God *allows* you to see, experience, or be a part of it, and you utilize *gossip* instead of the *gospel*. In exchange for life and all of its goodness, you are required to *ask* God into the situation as an intercessor or you will be held accountable and no longer trusted to see or hear. *Trust* is the key. You are *trusted* to see the IT, *troubled* until you *transform* IT, and *triumph* in the treasured *life in the second half!* After all scripture reminds us to whom much is given, much is required. *Life in the Second Half* is the opportunity to let the world know perseverance is productive and to not give up in the face of adversity. Strive for excellence in every endeavor you are involved in. You are the best you that will ever be made. Welcome to *Life in the Second Half*.

ACKNOWLEDGMENTS:

This book is dedicated in memory of all who have experienced *Life in the Second Half.*

To my parents: Thank you for giving me a first half and an opportunity at the second half.

To Bishop Dreyfus C. Smith: thank you for your friendship, mentorship, and spiritual guidance.

To Pastor Dr. Gregory L. Pollard: thank you for being you and empowering me to be me. God made me, Bishop put me together, I broke it and God, you, and Pastor Ellis picked up the pieces and put me back together.

To my personal Pastor, Walter E. Ellis: thank you and The Pilgrim Rest Family for accepting and embracing me.

To David Kelly Jackson III (Poppy): I've learned so much from you about myself. God birthed my joy on the day He loaned me you. I love you son.

To all my family and friends: over the years we've shared countless laughs, memories, joy, and tears. Thanks to each and every one of you. The best is yet to come.

To my Magnolia Baptist Church family: thank you all for trusting God and having faith in the process.

Thanks to my Heavenly Father, His Son, and precious Holy Spirit for the inspiration and protection you continually provide. Thank you all.

BIBLIOGRAPHY

Pg.6 Richard "Mr. Clean" Wright, *Except What God Allow* (song)

Pg.7 Mike Tyson, "Being Good is a Choice"

Pg. 11 Article written by Bob Sakamoto, *Chicago Tribune*

Pg. 13 African Pataki, "You better be running", author unknown

Pg. 17 "We know what history means to us, yet what will we mean to history" (Bishop Dreyfus C. Smith).

http://www.crosswalk.com/blogs/michael-craven/they-love-jesus-they-dont-like-the-church-11568526.html

http://www.huffingtonpost.com/2013/10/04/racial-dispari-ties-criminal-justice_n_4045144.html